·MATHEMATICS IN ACTION·

MATH
ANTHOLOGY
STORIES
& POEMS

GRADE 5

MACMILLAN / McGRAW-HILL
SCHOOL PUBLISHING COMPANY
New York   Columbus

The **MATH ANTHOLOGY Stories and Poems** offers a variety of traditional and contemporary selections of children's literature. These selections are used as the basis for many of the individual and small-group activities in **MATHEMATICS IN ACTION.** Every story and poem is keyed to an activity in a specific lesson, and where applicable, the selections are correlated for use in other chapters.

MACMILLAN/McGRAW-HILL SCHOOL DIVISION
10 UNION SQUARE EAST, NEW YORK, NEW YORK 10003

Printed in the United States of America

ISBN 0-02-109299-0 / 5

1 2 3 4 5 6 7 8 9 BAW 99 98 97 96 95 94 93

Illustration Credits: Neverne Covington 24–28, 38–39, 40–42; David Diaz 11–14; Allan Eitzen 4–5, 31–35; Steve Henry 36; Steven Nau 2; Hima Pamoedjo 9–10; Joshua Schreier 29–30; Dorothea Sierra 3, 37, 43; Mei Wang 20–21; Bea Weidner 22–23; Ron Zalme 6–8

Cover Illustration: Zita Asbaghi

ACKNOWLEDGMENTS

The Publisher gratefully acknowledges permission to reprint the following copyrighted material:

Excerpt from MELISANDE by Edith Nesbit. Reprinted by permission of Harcourt Brace Jovanovich, Inc.

"Anansi and the Plantains" from ANANSI *The Spider Man* by Philip M. Sherlock. Copyright © 1954 by Philip M. Sherlock. Reprinted by permission of HarperCollins Publishers.

"Numbers" from ELEANOR FARJEON'S POEMS FOR CHILDREN by Eleanor Farjeon. Copyright © 1926, 1927, 1933, 1938, 1951 by Eleanor Farjeon. Reprinted by permission of HarperCollins Publishers.

"The Sticks of Truth" from STORIES TO SOLVE by George Shannon. Text copyright © 1985 by George Shannon. Reprinted by permission of Greenwillow Books, a division of William Morrow & Company, Inc.

Excerpt from "Distances" from JULIE BROWN RACING AGAINST THE WORLD by R. R. Knudson. Copyright © 1988 by R. R. Knudson. Used by permission of Viking Penguin, a division of Penguin Books USA Inc.

"Too Clever Is Not Clever," from A TREASURY OF JEWISH FOLKLORE edited by Nathan Ausubel. Copyright 1948, 1976 by Crown Publishers, Inc. Reprinted by permission of Crown Publishers, Inc.

"3. Don't Can It!" and "4. Precycle It!" from 50 SIMPLE THINGS KIDS CAN DO TO SAVE THE EARTH by EarthWorks Group. Copyright © 1990 by John Javna. Reprinted by permission of Universal Press Syndicate. All rights reserved.

"One Inch Tall" from WHERE THE SIDEWALK ENDS by Shel Silverstein. Copyright © 1974 by Shel Silverstein. Reprinted by permission of HarperCollins Publishers.

"I Don't Have the Words" from PRIDE OF PUERTO RICO: THE LIFE OF ROBERTO CLEMENTE by Paul Robert Walker. Copyright © 1988 by Harcourt Brace Jovanovich, Inc. Reprinted by permission of the publisher.

Chapter 8 from MAX MALONE MAKES A MILLION by Charlotte Herman. Copyright © 1991 by Charlotte Herman. Reprinted by permission of Henry Holt and Company, Inc.

(Acknowledgments continue on page 52)

•CONTENTS•

Numbers
a poem by Eleanor Farjeon **2**

Peter Anthony
a poem by Sandra Liatsos **3**

Too Clever Is Not Clever
a Jewish folktale retold by Nathan Ausubel **4**

Distances
a selection from the biography *Julie Brown: Racing Against the World*
by R. R. Knudson **6**

Sticks of Truth
a folktale from India retold by George Shannon **9**

I Don't Have the Words
a selection from the biography *Pride of Puerto Rico: The Life of Roberto Clemente*
by Paul Robert Walker **11**

Melisande
an excerpt from the fairy tale by E. Nesbit **15**

Halfway Up the Skies
an ancient Chinese fable translated by K. L. Kiu **20**

Don't Can It!
an activity from *50 Simple Things Kids Can Do to Save the Earth*
by the EarthWorks Group **22**

The Phantom Tollbooth
a selection from the book by Norton Juster   24

Precycle It!
an activity from *50 Simple Things Kids Can Do to Save the Earth*
by the EarthWorks Group   29

Baseballs for Sale
from *Max Malone Makes a Million* by Charlotte Herman   31

Said Mrs. Isosceles Tri
a poem by Clinton Brooks Burgess   36

Buying Shoes
an ancient Chinese fable translated by K. L. Kiu   37

Huckleberry and Cranberry Fritters
from *Spirit of Harvest: North American Indian Cooking*
by Beverly Cox and Martin Jacobs   38

Anansi and the Plantains
a West African folktale retold by Philip Sherlock   40

Bird Watching
a poem by Myra Cohn Livingston   43

One Inch Tall
a poem by Shel Silverstein   44

Index   45

USING THE ANTHOLOGY

This chart correlates the Anthology selections to the 1994 Grade 5 *Mathematics in Action* program. Boldface type indicates where the selection is used in the Teacher's Edition of the program.

SELECTION	PAGE	CHAPTER(S)
Numbers a poem	2	Chapter **1**
Peter Anthony a poem	3	Chapter **1**
Too Clever Is Not Clever a Jewish folktale	4	Chapters 2, 4, 5
Distances a selection from a biography	6	Chapters 2, 6, 9
Sticks of Truth a folktale from India	9	Chapters 2, 9
I Don't Have the Words a selection from a biography	11	Chapter 3
Melisande an excerpt from a fairy tale	15	Chapters 2, **4**, 9
Halfway Up the Skies an ancient Chinese fable	20	Chapters 4, 5
Don't Can It! an activity	22	Chapters 4, **5**

SELECTION	PAGE	CHAPTER(S)
The Phantom Tollbooth a selection from the book	**24**	Chapter **6**
Precycle It! an activity	**29**	Chapters **7**, 9
Baseballs for Sale a story	**31**	Chapter 7
Said Mrs. Isosceles Tri a poem	**36**	Chapter **8**
Buying Shoes an ancient Chinese fable	**37**	Chapters 2, **9**
Huckleberry and Cranberry Fritters Native American recipes	**38**	Chapter **10**
Anansi and the Plantains a West African folktale	**40**	Chapters 9, 10, **11**
Bird Watching a poem	**43**	Chapters 1, **12**
One Inch Tall a poem	**44**	Chapters 9, **12**

STORIES & POEMS

Numbers

BY ELEANOR FARJEON

From the numbers 0 (nought) through 9, hundreds and thousands and millions of other numbers can be made. As Eleanor Farjeon assures us in her poem, there are numbers to count anything and everything in the world.

There are hundreds of Numbers. They mount up so high,
That if you could count every star in the sky
From the Tail of the Bear to the Waterman's Hat,
There still would be even more Numbers than that!

There are thousands of Numbers. So many there be,
That if you could count every drop in the sea
From the Mexican Gulf to the Lincolnshire Flat,
There still would be even more Numbers than that!

There are millions of Numbers. So many to spare,
That if you could count every insect in air,
The moth, the mosquito, the bee and the gnat,
There still would be even more Numbers than that!

There's no end to Numbers! But don't be afraid!
There only are ten out of which they are made,
Learn from Nought up to Nine, and the rest will come pat,
For the numbers of Numbers all come out of that!

Peter Anthony

BY SANDRA LIATSOS

Peter Anthony has no trouble at all imagining a zillion zebras jumping on his bed or a thousand buffalo grazing in his yard. Creating their own number for a zillion will reinforce students' understanding of place value.

"I have a million alligators
swimming in my pool,"
says Peter Anthony
Paul Meridith O'Toole.
"I have a thousand buffalo
out grazing in my yard,"
says Peter Anthony, "I ride them
cause it isn't hard."
"A zillion zebras on my bed
are jumping right this minute,"
says Peter Anthony, "and I will
join them while they spin it."
He hurries off
and leaves me thinking
while I bounce my ball,
"Poor Peter Anthony. That kid
just cannot count at all."

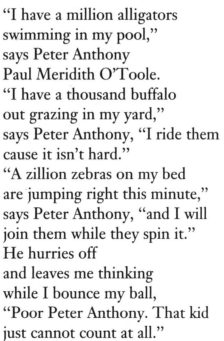

3

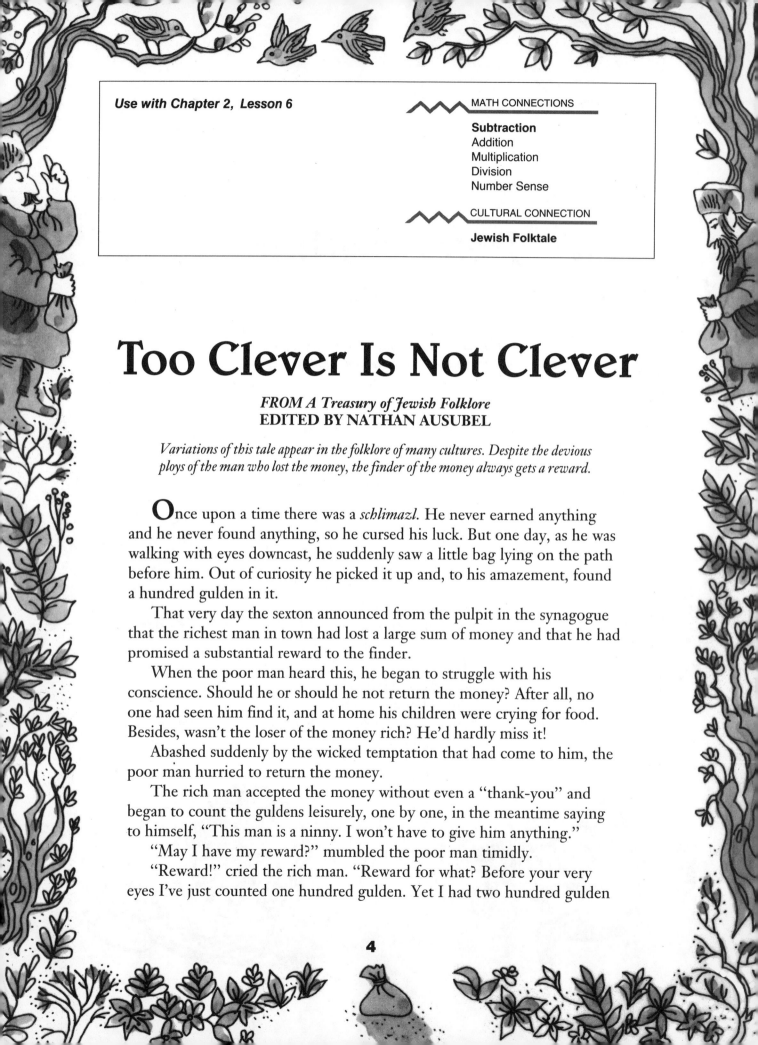

Use with Chapter 2, Lesson 6

MATH CONNECTIONS

Subtraction
Addition
Multiplication
Division
Number Sense

CULTURAL CONNECTION

Jewish Folktale

Too Clever Is Not Clever

FROM *A Treasury of Jewish Folklore*
EDITED BY NATHAN AUSUBEL

Variations of this tale appear in the folklore of many cultures. Despite the devious ploys of the man who lost the money, the finder of the money always gets a reward.

Once upon a time there was a *schlimazl*. He never earned anything and he never found anything, so he cursed his luck. But one day, as he was walking with eyes downcast, he suddenly saw a little bag lying on the path before him. Out of curiosity he picked it up and, to his amazement, found a hundred gulden in it.

That very day the sexton announced from the pulpit in the synagogue that the richest man in town had lost a large sum of money and that he had promised a substantial reward to the finder.

When the poor man heard this, he began to struggle with his conscience. Should he or should he not return the money? After all, no one had seen him find it, and at home his children were crying for food. Besides, wasn't the loser of the money rich? He'd hardly miss it!

Abashed suddenly by the wicked temptation that had come to him, the poor man hurried to return the money.

The rich man accepted the money without even a "thank-you" and began to count the guldens leisurely, one by one, in the meantime saying to himself, "This man is a ninny. I won't have to give him anything."

"May I have my reward?" mumbled the poor man timidly.

"Reward!" cried the rich man. "Reward for what? Before your very eyes I've just counted one hundred gulden. Yet I had two hundred gulden in that bag. Since you have already stolen a hundred you have some nerve to ask a reward."

"Then let us go to the rabbi," demanded the poor man.

"Very well," said the rich man.

The rabbi listened attentively to both men. Then he turned to the rich man and asked, "How much money was in the bag you lost?"

"Two hundred gulden."

"And how much money was in the bag you found?" asked the rabbi of the poor man.

"One hundred gulden."

"In that case," said the rabbi to the rich man, "the bag of money he found is not yours. I order you to give back the hundred gulden to this man!"

Distances

FROM Julie Brown Racing Against the World
BY R. R. KNUDSON

In addition to participating in the 1984 Olympics as a marathon runner, Julie Brown broke sprint records at UCLA. She was one of the first women to be awarded an athletic scholarship to attend college. This excerpt features some of Julie Brown's experiences while attending UCLA.

"**I** was so sure of her raw speed I'd've bet my house on Julie to win Olympic gold in the 800."

Coach Pat Connolly reached that conclusion after she had timed Julie on the UCLA track. Julie showed what she could do in the 100-meter dash, the 200, 400, and 800 meters. (Olympic distances are measured in meters rather than in yards; 800 meters is about half a mile.) Pat decided the 800-meter race was Julie's best distance. It combined Julie's foot speed with the endurance she had built in training.

Then, all of a sudden, Pat Connolly quit her job as coach. She wanted more time at home. The job was given to Chuck DeBus, coach of the Los Angeles Track Club (LATC). A tense, handsome young man, Chuck was totally devoted to winning. He had begun to earn a reputation as one of America's best coaches of women athletes. His reputation was based on the many medals they'd won and the many U.S. teams they'd been chosen for.

Racing was becoming more popular with women. Sports doctors were pointing out that women's health actually improved with vigorous exercise. Women themselves now insisted on running in longer races, even in marathons. Their coaches and lawyers backed them up. So did the United States Congress. It passed a law, called Title Nine for short, that required colleges to set aside equal amounts of money for men's and women's sports.

At long last! Women could win athletic scholarships. They'd get their tuition, room, and meals free, or rather, in exchange for their time playing on college teams.

Julie Brown received one of the very first athletic scholarships for women.

Not that she needed it. Her grandfather Brown had left money for her education. But Julie deserved to be supported by UCLA in the same way their football players were supported.

She began her freshman year in September 1973. Her days seemed to settle into an ordinary cycle of classes and exams and part-time jobs and sorority parties and then more classes. But not really! Those were just the surface events of her life. Underneath lay Julie's real life, her emotional life — her running.

That fall she ran in cross-country races. She raced two miles, sometimes three miles. Chuck DeBus had moved Julie way up past the 800 meters. He didn't agree it was her best distance.

He says, "It was apparent from her workouts that she could run longer, faster, and stay comfortable. I wrote her a note."

You will be a finalist in the 1976 Olympics in the 1,500 meters.

He meant his note to inspire Julie. The 1,500-meter race (about a mile) was then the longest women's race in the Olympics. Chuck made for Julie a training schedule that called for running 40, 50, 60, 70 miles a week. She ran these on the UCLA campus and along the streets of Santa Monica to the Pacific Ocean and back. She ran the hills of Bel Air. She ran tree-shaded paths in Beverly Hills. Often the UCLA teammates ran together. Other days, Julie ran with Chuck or alone.

Speed is increased not only by running *long* distances at less than top speed but also by sprinting short distances as fast as possible. Several times a week Chuck met his team at the UCLA track. He held the stopwatch and shouted each second ticking away as Julie circled in 66 seconds, 65, 64. Even while sprinting, she moved smoothly, "almost like a cat," according to Chuck. She was so much faster than her teammates that there was little jealousy about her position as the team's star. She was as modest — silent — about her accomplishments as she had been in Montana.

For a college freshman, Julie had a fantastic cross-country season. She took third place at the AAU national cross-country race. This earned her a place on the U.S. team, which flew to Italy for the world cross-country championship. There Julie disappointed herself by finishing 27th.

"I was lagged out," she explains in athletes' slang. They mean they get hours behind in sleep by jetting across time zones.

She came right back for the spring track season. Each race she won scored points for the UCLA team. In some meets she ran four different distances. She helped her team take second place at the college championships by running the half mile, the mile, the two-mile, and finally a quarter mile of a relay race. Later in the season she set an American outdoor record in the three miles — 16:08.

For many students, their freshman year, when they are freshly enthusiastic, brings greater success than their second year at college. Not so with Julie. She'd decided to major in kinesiology (say "kin-EES-ee-OL-o-gee"), which is the science of body movement. She kept up a B average in her classes.

Julie moved into a sorority house. She was known there as a caring, thoughtful "sister" who sometimes came late to dinner or missed it completely because she was running around — the track, that is! She was training for a spectacular year of racing.

During the winter she raced on indoor tracks. These were set up in huge basketball arenas. At Madison Square Garden in New York City Julie ran the mile in 4:43. She improved her time to 4:41 when she raced in the Russian-American indoor track meet in Richmond, Virginia. She enjoyed traveling.

Julie flew across half the world to race in Rabat, Morocco. It was blistering hot there for the world cross-country championship. She arrived several days early to make up for jet lag.

"All I did was sleep, eat, sleep, run a workout, sleep, sleep. I slept 15 hours a day before the race," Julie remembers.

The racecourse had been laid out on the infield of a horse racetrack. There were bales of hay to jump and rough dirt underfoot. A crowd of 10,000, including the rulers of Morocco, watched from the grandstand.

Julie went to the front of the race as soon as she could work her way through the crowd of 70 women. Then she kept them all behind her by pouring on speed. She surefootedly jumped the hay bales. She glided over the mud. Her footfalls were so light they scarcely left a print. She won the race and became the world champion, only 20 years old.

Use with Chapter 2, Lesson 12

MATH CONNECTIONS
Time
Measurement

CULTURAL CONNECTION
Folktale from India

The Sticks of Truth

FROM Stories to Solve
BY GEORGE SHANNON

Using sticks of truth, a wise judge traps a thief. This folktale also can be used to discuss customary and metric units of measurement.

Long ago in India judges traveled from village to village. One day a judge stopped at an inn to rest, but the innkeeper was very upset. Someone had just that day stolen his daughter's gold ring. The judge told him not to worry and had all the guests gather so that he could question them. When he could not figure out from their answers who the thief was, the judge decided to use some old magic. He told them all he was going to have to use the sticks of truth.

"These are magic sticks," he explained, "that will catch the thief."

He gave each guest a stick to keep under their bed during the night.

"The stick belonging to the thief will grow two inches during the night. At breakfast we will all compare sticks and the longest stick will be the thief's."

The next morning the judge had all the guests come by his table and hold their sticks up next to his to see if they had grown. But one after another all were the same. None of them had grown any longer. Then suddenly the judge called, "This is the thief! Her stick is shorter than all the rest."

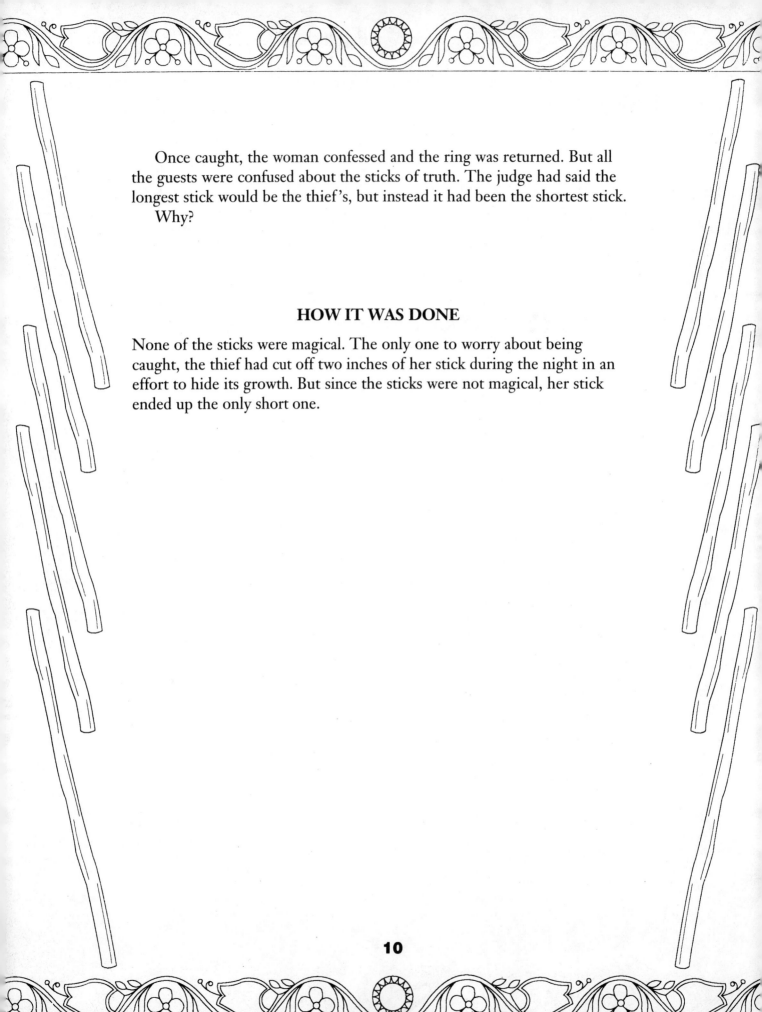

Once caught, the woman confessed and the ring was returned. But all the guests were confused about the sticks of truth. The judge had said the longest stick would be the thief's, but instead it had been the shortest stick. Why?

HOW IT WAS DONE

None of the sticks were magical. The only one to worry about being caught, the thief had cut off two inches of her stick during the night in an effort to hide its growth. But since the sticks were not magical, her stick ended up the only short one.

Use with Chapter 3, Lesson 11

MATH CONNECTIONS

Decimals
Subtraction
Addition

CULTURAL CONNECTION

**Puerto Rican
Biography**

I Don't Have the Words

FROM Pride of Puerto Rico
The Life of Roberto Clemente
BY PAUL ROBERT WALKER

Roberto Clemente (1934-1972) was an outfielder for the Pittsburgh Pirates. He won the National League's batting championship four times. During the off-season, Clemente lived in his native Puerto Rico. He died in a plane crash on his way to aid earthquake victims in Nicaragua.

On June 28, 1970, the Pittsburgh Pirates played their last game at Forbes Field. For Roberto, it was an emotional moment. "I spent half my life there," he said. Two and a half weeks later, after a long road trip, the team moved into their new home at Three Rivers Stadium.

Built at the junction of the Ohio, Allegheny, and Monongahela rivers, the new park was an ultramodern stadium with an evenly shaped field and artificial turf. After sixteen years of playing on grass, Roberto quickly adapted to the new surface. On a ball hit into the gap between right and center field, he'd slide on the carpet, pick up the ball, and spring to his feet to make the throw all in one graceful motion.

The Pirates seemed to like their new home as well. The year before, the National League had been divided into two divisions. In their first two weeks at Three Rivers, the Pirates passed the New York Mets and took over first place in the National League East.

On July 24, the Pirates were scheduled to play the Houston Astros. Before the game, Roberto stood on the new green carpet and looked around the stadium. There were over 43,000 fans. In the right-field stands, he could see hundreds of *pavas*, the big white straw hats worn by Puerto Rican workers in the sugar fields. The people of Puerto Rico had come to join the people of Pittsburgh in his honor. It was Roberto Clemente Night.

On the field with Roberto were Vera and their three children, Roberto Jr., Luis, and tiny Enrique. Doña Luisa and Don Melchor sat beside them. Don Melchor was ninety years old now. He was thin and frail, but his eyes were still strong and clear. The trip to Pittsburgh was his first time on an airplane.

Heriberto Nieves, the mayor of Carolina, also sat on the field in honor of his city's most famous son. There were other officials from Puerto Rico and many important citizens of Pittsburgh. The entire program was broadcast by satellite to Puerto Rico.

As the ceremony began, the other Latin players on the Pirates walked up to Roberto in single file. Each placed a hand on his shoulder and bent forward in an *abrazo*, an embrace. A young Puerto Rican businessman named Juan Jiménez presented Roberto with a scroll containing 300,000 signatures from the people of Puerto Rico. Out of a population of around 3,000,000, one out of every ten Puerto Ricans had signed the scroll.

Roberto was presented with many other gifts and trophies, including a brand-new car. At Roberto's request, thousands of dollars were donated to help the crippled children at Pittsburgh's Children's Hospital. Finally, it came time for Roberto to speak. The announcer, Ramiro Martínez, asked him to say a few words in Spanish to the people who were watching and listening in Puerto Rico.

"Before anything," Roberto began, "I want to send an *abrazo* to my brothers . . ." Suddenly he turned away from the microphone. His eyes were wet with tears. Martínez whispered some words of encouragement. After a few moments, Roberto continued.

"I want to dedicate this triumph to all the mothers in Puerto Rico. I haven't the words to express my gratitude. I only ask that those who are watching this program be close to their parents, ask for their blessing and embrace . . . and those friends who are watching or listening, shake hands in the friendship that unites all Puerto Ricans."

When he was finished, Roberto looked over at his mother and his father. There were tears in their eyes and tears in his eyes, too. There, in front of 43,000 people and tens of thousands more watching on television, Roberto did not have to say another word to show the love and respect he felt for Don Melchor and Doña Luisa.

Now it was time for the game. Before the "Star-Spangled Banner," the fans and players stood for "La Borinqueña," the national anthem of Puerto Rico. As the Astros came up to bat in the first inning, the Puerto Rican fans in right field serenaded Roberto with a special song written just for that night. "Roberto Clemente, orgulla de Puerto Rico," it began. "Roberto Clemente, the pride of Puerto Rico."

Behind the great pitching of Dock Ellis, the Pirates routed the Astros 11-0. Roberto had two hits and made a fantastic sliding catch in right field. Late in the game, with the Pirates already on their way to an easy win, Robert made another diving catch of a foul ball. As he stood to his feet, there was blood seeping through the knee of his uniform pants. Later, when reporters asked him why he risked hurting himself on a play that didn't really matter, he shrugged and said, "It's the only way I know how to play baseball."

With two out in the top of the ninth inning, Manager Danny Murtaugh removed Roberto from the game. Murtaugh had returned at the beginning of the season for his third turn as the Pirate manager. This time there were no conflicts between the tough manager and his fiery superstar. As Roberto trotted in from right field, the fans showed their appreciation with a standing ovation. In the Pirate dugout, Murtaugh stood and applauded with them.

After the game, a reporter asked Roberto about his tears during the ceremony. "In a moment like this," he said, "you can see a lot of years in a few minutes. You can see everything firm and you can see everything clear. I don't know if I cried, but I am not ashamed to cry. I would say a man never cries from pain or disappointment. But if you know the history of our island, you ought to remember we're a sentimental people. I don't have the words to say how I feel when I step on that field and know that so many are behind me, and know that so many represent my island and Latin America."

Roberto had a number of injuries during the 1970 season. But when Danny Murtaugh tried to rest him on the bench, he kept on playing. "I wanted to rest him," Murtaugh said, "but he insisted on playing because we haven't been winning. He's doing everything he can to get us rolling."

Years before, it was Murtaugh who demanded that Roberto play with injuries. Now it was Roberto who refused to rest. Times had changed.

In late August, the Pirates were playing the Dodgers in Los Angeles. During a long 16-inning game, Roberto had five hits in seven at-bats. He drove in one run and scored another as the Bucs finally edged the Dodgers 2-1. The next night, the Pirates had an easier time, beating the Dodgers 11-0. Again Roberto had five hits, including a double and a home run. It was the first time in modern baseball history that a player had ten hits in two consecutive games.

After his record-breaking performance, Roberto led the National League with an average of .363. But in early September, he reinjured his

13

back while swinging too hard at a pitch. By the end of the season, his average had dropped slightly to .352. The Pirates, with Danny Murtaugh back in charge, won the National League East but lost to the Cincinnati Reds in the divisional playoffs. The World Series would have to wait.

After the season, Roberto was asked if he still wanted to retire. He was 36 years old now, and many players his age had given up the game long ago. "Let's see," he said with a smile. "I hit .345 last year and .352 this year. No, I don't think I want to quit now."

Roberto looked at the men who had come to see him at his home in Río Piedras. It was January of 1971, and he was busy managing the San Juan Senators in the winter league. Even though he had five of his Pirate teammates playing for him in Puerto Rico, the team was struggling. But that was a different problem. Now there was something else on his mind.

"Roberto," said one of the men, "we are here to ask you a great favor. You are a respected citizen and a fine man. Time and time again, you have proven your love for the people of Puerto Rico. We need a man with your intelligence and leadership. We want you to run for mayor of Carolina."

Roberto listened respectfully to the man's words. He considered the offer. Certainly he was popular enough in Carolina to win the election. As mayor he could do many things to help his people. But the more he thought about it, the more he was sure that he did not have the personality for politics. He would have to help in other ways.

"There's no use for me to say yes," he said. "Say I was elected and a situation came up where I have to compromise. I cannot compromise."

That winter, Roberto had other concerns as well. Don Melchor fell seriously ill and had to have surgery. Before the operation, Roberto sat at his father's bedside, looking down at his worn and tired face. It is only on the outside that he is old, Roberto thought. On the inside, his heart is young.

Don Melchor looked weakly up at his son. Over the years, he had learned much more about baseball. He knew that the Pirates had come very close in 1970. And he knew that Roberto wanted to play in one more World Series before he retired. "Momen," he said, "you can make it better this year."

Roberto smiled. He appreciated Don Melchor's encouragement, but his father's health was more important to him than the World Series. "No, Papá," he said, "you go and make it better this year."

Melisande

An Excerpt From the Book
BY E. NESBIT

A curse has made the Princess Melisande bald, but a wish gives her more hair than she imagined—hair a yard long that grows an inch every day and then grows twice as fast each time it's cut.

*W*hen the Princess Melisande was born, her mother, the Queen, wished to have a christening party, but the King put his foot down and said he would not have it.

"I've seen too much trouble come of christening parties," said he. "However carefully you keep your visiting book, some fairy or other is sure to get left out, and you know what *that* leads to. Why, even in my own family the most shocking things have occurred. The fairy Malevola was not asked to my great-grandmother's christening, and you know all about the spindle and the hundred years' sleep."

"Perhaps you're right," said the Queen. "My own cousin by marriage forgot a stuffy old fairy when she sent out the cards for her daughter's christening, and the old wretch turned up at the last moment. The girl drops toads out of her mouth to this day."

"Exactly. And then there was that business of the mouse and the kitchen maids," said the King. "We'll have no nonsense about it. I'll be her godfather, and you shall be her godmother, and we won't ask a single fairy. Then none of them can be offended."

"Unless they all are," said the Queen.

And that was exactly what happened. When the King and the Queen and the baby got back from the christening, the parlormaid met them at the door and said, "Please, Your Majesty, several ladies have called. I told them you were not at home, but they all said they'd wait."

15

"Are they in the parlor?" asked the Queen.

"I've shown them into the Throne Room, Your Majesty," said the parlormaid. "You see, there are several of them."

There were in fact seven hundred. The great Throne Room was crammed with fairies of all ages and of all degrees of beauty and ugliness: good fairies and bad fairies, flower fairies and moon fairies, fairies like spiders and fairies like butterflies. As the Queen opened the door and began to say how sorry she was to have kept them waiting, they all cried with one voice, "Why didn't you ask me to your christening party?"

"I haven't had a party," said the Queen. She turned to the King and whispered, "I told you so." This was her only consolation.

"You've had a christening," said the fairies all together.

"I'm very sorry . . ." began the poor Queen, but Malevola pushed forward and said, "Hold your tongue," most rudely.

Malevola is the oldest, as well as the most wicked, of the fairies. She is deservedly unpopular and has been left out of more christening parties than all the rest of the fairies put together.

"Don't make excuses," she said, shaking her finger at the Queen. "That only makes your conduct worse. You know well enough what happens if a fairy is left out of a christening party. We are all going to give our christening presents *now*. As the fairy of highest social position, I shall begin. The Princess shall be bald."

The Queen nearly fainted as Malevola drew back. Another fairy, in a stylish hat with snakes on it, stepped forward with a rustle of bats' wings.

But the King stepped forward too. "No, you don't!" said he. "I wonder at you, ladies, I do indeed. How can you be so unfairylike? Have none of you been to school? Have none of you studied the history of your own race? Surely you don't need a poor, ignorant King like me to tell you that this is *no go?*"

"How dare you?" cried the fairy in the hat, and the snakes quivered as she tossed her head. "It is my turn, and I say that the Princess shall be . . ."

The King actually put his hand over her mouth.

"Look here," he said, "I won't have it. Listen to reason or you'll be sorry afterward. A fairy who breaks the traditions of fairy history goes out — you know she does — like the flame of a candle. And all tradition shows that only *one* bad fairy is ever forgotten at a christening party and the good ones are always invited. So either this is not a christening party, or else you were all invited except one, and, by her own showing, that was Malevola. It nearly always is. Do I make myself clear?"

Several of the higher-ranking fairies who had been influenced by Malevola murmured that there was something in what His Majesty said.

"Try it, if you don't believe me," said the King. "Give your nasty gifts to my innocent child. But as sure as you do, out you go, like a candle flame. Now then, will you risk it?"

No one answered, and presently several fairies came up to the Queen and said what a pleasant party it had been but they really must be going. This example decided the rest. One by one all the fairies said good-bye and thanked the Queen for the delightful afternoon they had spent with her.

"It's been quite too lovely," said the lady with the snake hat. "Do ask us again soon, dear Queen. I shall be so *longing* to see you again and the *dear* baby." And off she went, with the snake trimming quivering more wildly than ever.

When the very last fairy had gone the Queen ran to look at the baby. She tore off its lace cap and burst into tears, for all the baby's downy golden hair came off with the cap, and the Princess Melisande was bald as an egg.

"Don't cry, my love," said the King. "I have a wish lying around that I've never had occasion to use. My fairy godmother gave it to me for a wedding present, but since then I've had nothing to wish for!"

"Thank you, dear," said the Queen, smiling through her tears.

"I'll keep the wish till baby grows up," the King went on. "And then I'll give it to her, and if she wants to wish for hair she can."

"Oh, won't you wish for it *now?*" said the Queen, dropping tears and kisses on the baby's round, smooth head.

"No, dearest. She may want something else even more when she grows up. And besides, her hair may grow by itself."

But it never did. Princess Melisande grew up as beautiful as the sun and as good as gold, but never a hair grew on that little head of hers. The Queen sewed her little caps of green silk, and the Princess's pink and white face looked out of them like a flower peeping out of its bud. And every day as she grew older she grew dearer, and as she grew dearer she grew better, and as she grew more good she grew more beautiful.

Now, when she had grown up, the Queen said to the King, "My love, our dear daughter is old enough to know what she wants. Let her have the wish."

So the King wrote to his fairy godmother and sent the letter by a butterfly. He asked if he might hand on to his daughter the wish the fairy had given him for a wedding present.

"I have never had occasion to use it," said he, "though it has always made me happy to remember that I had such a thing in the house. The wish is as good as new, and my daughter is now of an age to appreciate so valuable a present."

To which the fairy replied by return of butterfly:

Dear King,
Pray do whatever you like with my poor little present. I had quite forgotten it, but I am pleased to think that you have treasured my humble keepsake all these years.

Your affectionate godmother,
Fortuna F.

So the King unlocked his gold safe with the seven diamond-handled keys that hung at his girdle, took out the wish, and gave it to his daughter.

And Melisande said, "Father, I will wish that all your subjects should be quite happy."

But they were that already, because the King and Queen were so good. So the wish did not work.

So then she said, "Then I wish them all to be good."

But they were that already, because they were happy. So again the wish fell flat.

Then the Queen said, "Dearest, for my sake, wish what I tell you to." "Why, of course I will," said Melisande. The Queen whispered in her ear, and Melisande nodded. Then she said, "I wish I had golden hair a yard long, and that it would grow an inch every day, and grow twice as fast every time it was cut, and . . ."

"Stop!" cried the King. And the wish worked, for the next moment the Princess stood smiling at him through a shower of golden hair.

"Oh, how lovely," said the Queen. "What a pity you interrupted her, dear. She hadn't finished."

"What was the end?" asked the King.

"Oh," said Melisande, "I was only going to say, 'and twice as thick.' "

"It's a very good thing you didn't," said the King. "You've done about enough." For he had a mathematical mind and could do the sums about the grains of wheat on the chessboard and the nails in the horses' shoes in his royal head without any trouble at all.

"Why, what's the matter?" asked the Queen.

"You'll know soon enough, " said the King. "Come, let's be happy while we may. Give me a kiss, little Melisande, and then go to Nurse and ask her to teach you how to comb your hair."

"I know how," said Melisande. "I've often combed Mother's."

"Your mother has beautiful hair," said the King, "but I fancy you will find your own less easy to manage." And indeed it was so. The Princess's hair began by being a yard long, and it grew an inch every night. If you know anything at all about even the simplest sums, you will see that in about five weeks her hair was about two yards long. This is a very inconvenient length. It trails on the floor and sweeps up all the dust. And though in palaces, of course, it is all gold-dust, still it is not nice to have it in your hair. And the Princess's hair was growing an inch every night. When it was three yards long, the Princess could not bear it any longer, it was so heavy and so hot, so she borrowed Nurse's scissors and cut it all off, and then for a few hours she was comfortable. But the hair went on growing, and now it grew twice as fast as before so that in thirty-six days it was as long as ever. The poor Princess cried with tiredness, and when she couldn't bear it any more she cut her hair and was comfortable for a very little time. The hair now grew four times as fast as at first, and in eighteen days it was as long as before, and she had to have it cut. Then it grew eight inches a day, and the next time it was cut it grew sixteen inches a day, and then thirty-two inches and sixty-four inches and a hundred and twenty-eight inches a day, and so on, growing twice as fast after each cutting. The Princess would go to bed at night with her hair clipped short, and wake up in the morning with yards and yards and yards of golden hair flowing all around the room, so that she could not move without pulling her own hair and Nurse had to come and cut the hair off before she could get out of bed.

"I wish I were bald again," sighed poor Melisande, looking at the little green caps she used to wear, and she cried herself to sleep at night between the golden billows of the golden hair. But she never let her mother see her cry, because it was the Queen's fault and Melisande did not want to seem to reproach her. . . .

Use with Chapter 4, Lesson 14

MATH CONNECTIONS

Geometry
Multiplication
Division

CULTURAL CONNECTION

Chinese Fable

Halfway Up the Skies

FROM 100 Ancient Chinese Fables
TRANSLATED BY K. L. KIU

This fable serves as an introduction to circumference and its practical applications in the world. In imagining a tower halfway up the sky, the king's eyes were turned toward the sky when they should have been focused on the ground.

When the king of Wei decided to build a tower that would reach halfway up the skies, he gave an order: "Anyone who tries to dissuade me will be put to death."

Xu Wan, a minister of Wei, came to the presence of the king, carrying a dirt basket on his back and holding a spade in his hand.

"Sire, I heard that you are about to build a tower that would reach halfway up the skies," said Xu, "your humble servant would like to offer a helping hand."

"What strength have you got to offer?" asked the king.

"I may be lacking in strength," replied Xu, "but I can help in the planning of this construction."

"Well?" inquired the king.

"Sire, I have heard the distance between heaven and earth is fifteen thousand *li*. Now since you want to build a tower that reaches midway up the skies, the tower should be seven thousand five hundred *li* tall. With a structure that tall, the foundations must have a circumference of eight thousand *li*. Not all your lands together, sire, is enough for the foundations. In ancient times, the monarchs Yao and Shun established dukedoms which had a circumference of five thousand *li*. If you are determined to build this tower, you must first attack the dukes and take over all their lands. That is still not enough. You must also subdue the various barbarous tribes living in the far away regions to our north, south, east and west. When you have got an area with a boundary of eight thousand *li*, it will be adequate for the foundations. As for building materials, workers and stores of food, all these must be calculated by hundreds of millions. Outside the area bound by eight thousand *li*, a large number of fields must be designated for producing food to feed the workers constructing the tower. When all the conditions for building the tower are met, the work can begin."

The king was silent, unable to think of a reply. He gave up the idea of building the tower.

Xinxu

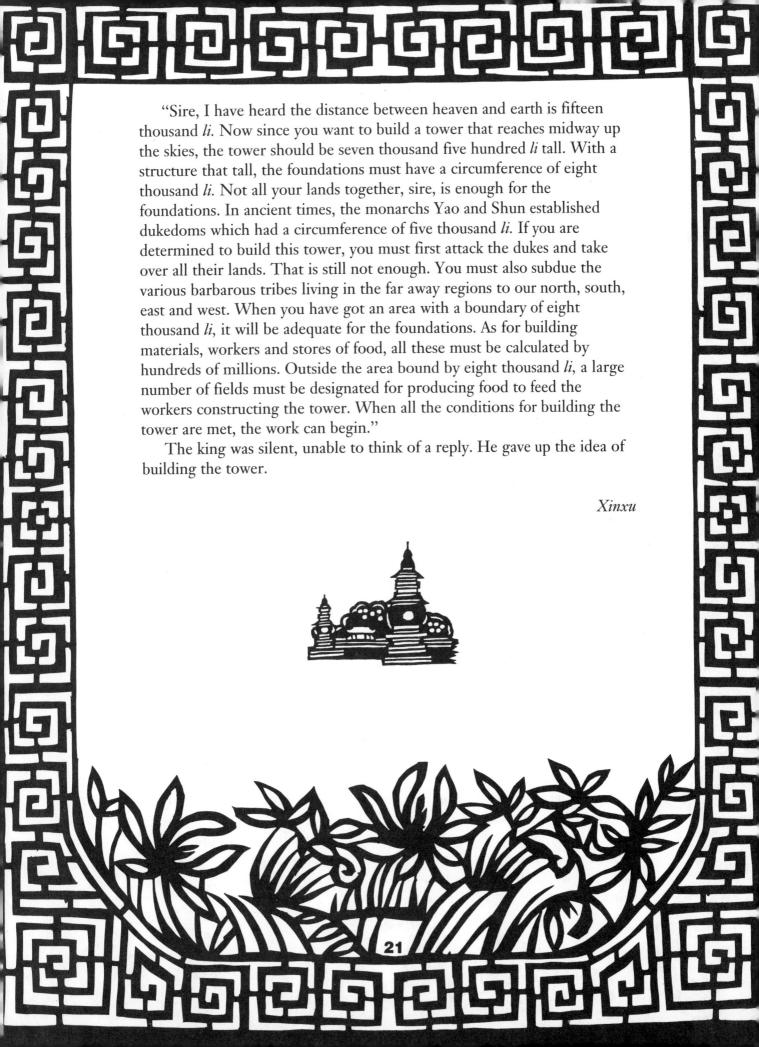

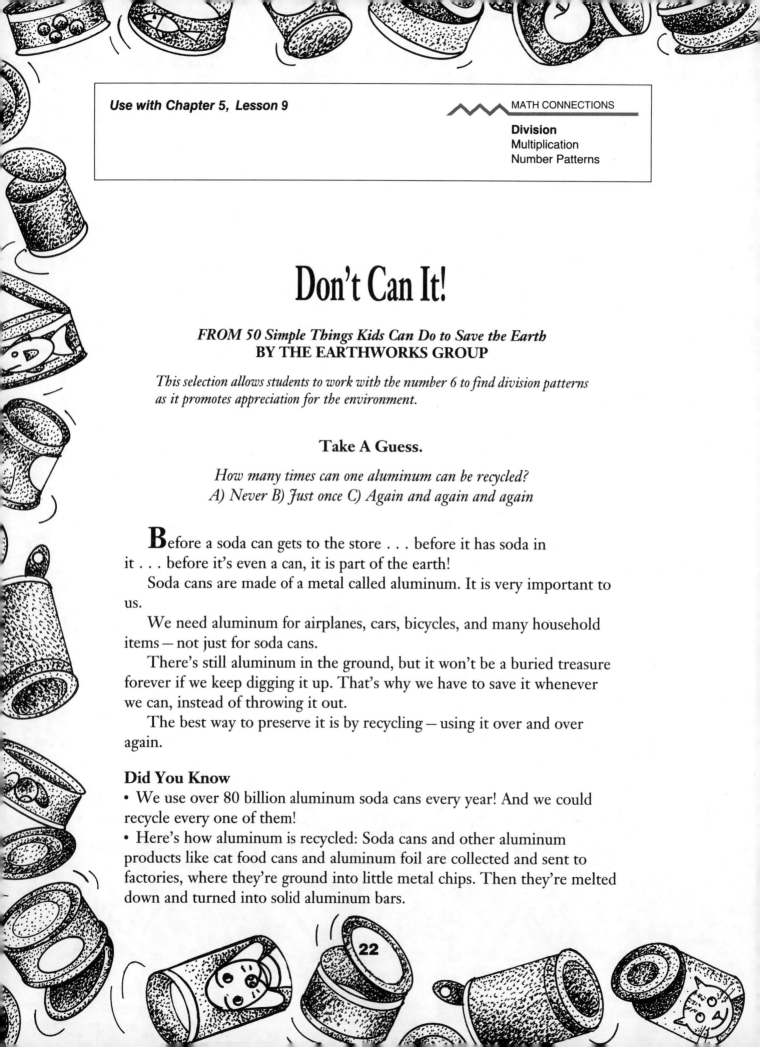

Don't Can It!

FROM 50 Simple Things Kids Can Do to Save the Earth
BY THE EARTHWORKS GROUP

This selection allows students to work with the number 6 to find division patterns as it promotes appreciation for the environment.

Take A Guess.

How many times can one aluminum can be recycled?
A) Never B) Just once C) Again and again and again

Before a soda can gets to the store . . . before it has soda in it . . . before it's even a can, it is part of the earth!

Soda cans are made of a metal called aluminum. It is very important to us.

We need aluminum for airplanes, cars, bicycles, and many household items — not just for soda cans.

There's still aluminum in the ground, but it won't be a buried treasure forever if we keep digging it up. That's why we have to save it whenever we can, instead of throwing it out.

The best way to preserve it is by recycling — using it over and over again.

Did You Know
• We use over 80 billion aluminum soda cans every year! And we could recycle every one of them!
• Here's how aluminum is recycled: Soda cans and other aluminum products like cat food cans and aluminum foil are collected and sent to factories, where they're ground into little metal chips. Then they're melted down and turned into solid aluminum bars.

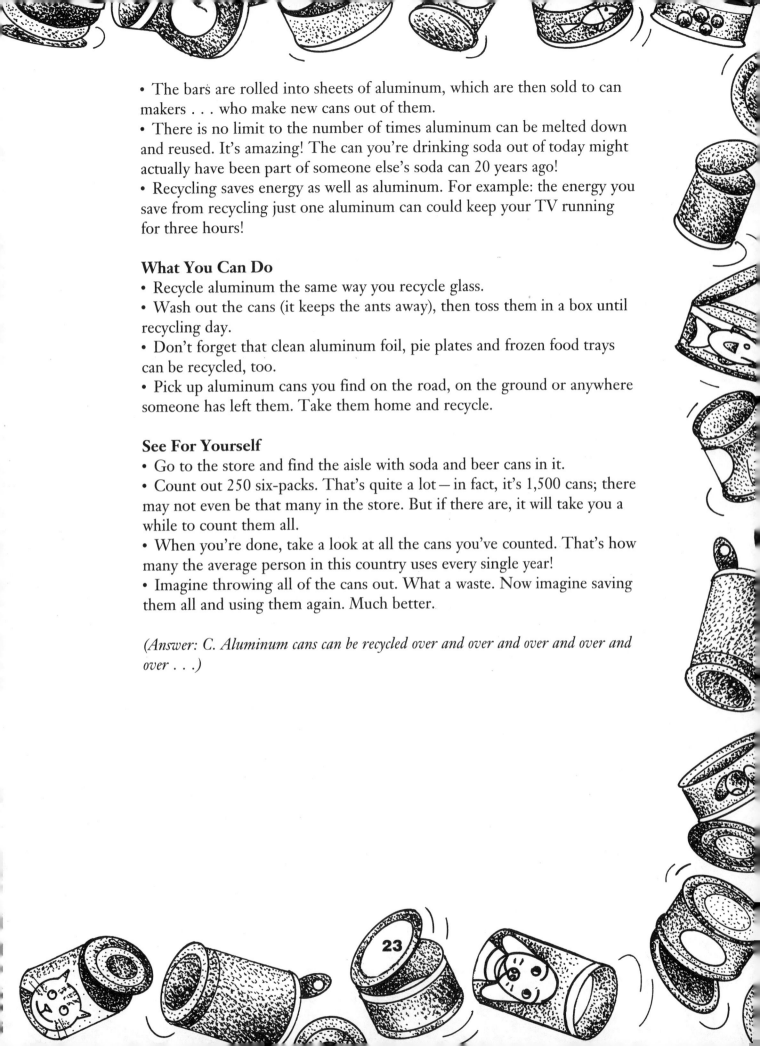

- The bars are rolled into sheets of aluminum, which are then sold to can makers . . . who make new cans out of them.
- There is no limit to the number of times aluminum can be melted down and reused. It's amazing! The can you're drinking soda out of today might actually have been part of someone else's soda can 20 years ago!
- Recycling saves energy as well as aluminum. For example: the energy you save from recycling just one aluminum can could keep your TV running for three hours!

What You Can Do
- Recycle aluminum the same way you recycle glass.
- Wash out the cans (it keeps the ants away), then toss them in a box until recycling day.
- Don't forget that clean aluminum foil, pie plates and frozen food trays can be recycled, too.
- Pick up aluminum cans you find on the road, on the ground or anywhere someone has left them. Take them home and recycle.

See For Yourself
- Go to the store and find the aisle with soda and beer cans in it.
- Count out 250 six-packs. That's quite a lot — in fact, it's 1,500 cans; there may not even be that many in the store. But if there are, it will take you a while to count them all.
- When you're done, take a look at all the cans you've counted. That's how many the average person in this country uses every single year!
- Imagine throwing all of the cans out. What a waste. Now imagine saving them all and using them again. Much better.

(Answer: C. Aluminum cans can be recycled over and over and over and over and over . . .)

23

THE PHANTOM TOLLBOOTH

Selections from "A Colorful Symphony/Discord and Dynne"
BY NORTON JUSTER

Milo's boredom disappears when he passes through the Phantom Tollbooth. In this selection, he attends a symphony that has at least a thousand musicians and is given the responsibility for waking all its members the next morning.

A Colorful Symphony

. . .**T**he sun was dropping slowly from sight, and stripes of purple and orange and crimson and gold piled themselves on top of the distant hills. The last shafts of light waited patiently for a flight of wrens to find their way home, and a group of anxious stars had already taken their places.

"Here we are!" cried Alec, and, with a sweep of his arm, he pointed toward an enormous symphony orchestra. "Isn't it a grand sight?"

There were at least a thousand musicians ranged in a great arc before them. To the left and right were the violins and cellos, whose bows moved in great waves, and behind them in numberless profusion the piccolos, flutes, clarinets, oboes, bassoons, horns, trumpets, trombones, and tubas were all playing at once. At the very rear, so far away that they could hardly be seen, were the percussion instruments, and lastly, in a long line up one side of a steep slope, were the solemn bass fiddles.

On a high podium in front stood the conductor, a tall, gaunt man with dark deep-set eyes and a thin mouth placed carelessly between his long pointed nose and his long pointed chin. He used no baton, but conducted with large, sweeping movements which seemed to start at his toes and work slowly up through his body and along his slender arms and end finally at the tips of his graceful fingers.

24

"I don't hear any music," said Milo.

"That's right," said Alec; "you don't listen to this concert—you watch it. Now, pay attention."

As the conductor waved his arms, he molded the air like handfuls of soft clay, and the musicians carefully followed his every direction.

"What are they playing?" asked Tock, looking up inquisitively at Alec.

"The sunset, of course. They play it every evening, about this time."

"They do?" said Milo quizzically.

"Naturally," answered Alec; "and they also play morning, noon, and night, when, of course, it's morning, noon, or night. Why, there wouldn't be any color in the world unless they played it. Each instrument plays a different one," he explained, "and depending, of course, on what season it is and how the weather's to be, the conductor chooses his score and directs the day. But watch: the sun has almost set, and in a moment you can ask Chroma himself."

The last colors slowly faded from the western sky, and, as they did, one by one the instruments stopped, until only the bass fiddles, in their somber slow movement, were left to play the night and a single set of silver bells brightened the constellations. The conductor let his arms fall limply at his sides and stood quite still as darkness claimed the forest.

"That was a very beautiful sunset," said Milo, walking to the podium.

"It should be," was the reply; "we've been practicing since the world began." And, reaching down, the speaker picked Milo off the ground and set him on the music stand. "I am Chroma the Great," he continued, gesturing broadly with his hands, "conductor of color, maestro of pigment, and director of the entire spectrum."

"Do you play all day long?" asked Milo when he had introduced himself.

"Ah yes, all day, every day," he sang out, then pirouetted gracefully around the platform. "I rest only at night, and even then *they* play on."

"What would happen if you stopped?" asked Milo, who didn't quite believe that color happened that way.

"See for yourself," roared Chroma, and he raised both hands high over his head. Immediately the instruments that were playing stopped, and at once all color vanished. The world looked like an enormous coloring book that had never been used. Everything appeared in simple black outlines, and it looked as if someone with a set of paints the size of a house and a brush as wide could stay happily occupied for years. Then Chroma lowered his arms. The instruments began again and the color returned.

"You see what a dull place the world would be without color?" he said, bowing until his chin almost touched the ground. "But what pleasure to lead my violins in a serenade of spring green or hear my trumpets blare out the blue sea and then watch the oboes tint it all in warm yellow sunshine. And rainbows are best of all—and blazing neon signs, and taxicabs with stripes, and the soft, muted tones of a foggy day. We play them all."

As Chroma spoke, Milo sat with his eyes open wide, and Alec, Tock, and the Humbug looked on in wonder.

"Now I really must get some sleep." Chroma yawned. "We've had lightning, fireworks, and parades for the last few nights, and I've had to be up to conduct them. But tonight is sure to be quiet." Then, putting his large hand on Milo's shoulder, he said, "Be a good fellow and watch my orchestra till morning, will you? And be sure to wake me at 5:23 for the sunrise. Good night, good night, good night."

With that he leaped lightly from the podium and, in three long steps, vanished into the forest.

"That's a good idea," said Tock, making himself comfortable in the grass as the bug grumbled himself quickly to sleep and Alec stretched out in mid-air.

And Milo, full of thoughts and questions, curled up on the pages of tomorrow's music and eagerly awaited the dawn.

Dischord and Dynne

One by one, the hours passed, and at exactly 5:22 (by Tock's very accurate clock) Milo carefully opened one eye and, in a moment, the other. Everything was still purple, dark blue, and black, yet scarcely a minute remained to the long, quiet night.

He stretched lazily, rubbed his eyelids, scratched his head, and shivered once as a greeting to the early-morning mist.

"I must wake Chroma for the sunrise," he said softly. Then he suddenly wondered what it would be like to lead the orchestra and to color the whole world himself.

The idea whirled through his thoughts until he quickly decided that since it couldn't be very difficult, and since they probably all knew what to do by themselves anyway, and since it did seem a shame to wake anyone so early, and since it might be his only chance to try, and since the musicians were already poised and ready, he would—but just for a little while.

And so, as everyone slept peacefully on, Milo stood on tiptoes, raised his arms slowly in front of him, and made the slightest movement possible with the index finger of his right hand. It was now 5:23 A.M.

As if understanding his signal perfectly, a single piccolo played a single note and off in the east a solitary shaft of cool lemon light flicked across the sky. Milo smiled happily and then cautiously crooked his finger again.

This time two more piccolos and a flute joined in and three more rays of light danced lightly into view. Then with both hands he made a great circular sweep in the air and watched with delight as all the musicians began to play at once.

The cellos made the hills glow red, and the leaves and grass were tipped with a soft pale green as the violins began their song. Only the bass fiddles rested as the entire orchestra washed the forest in color.

Milo was overjoyed because they were all playing for him, and just the way they should.

"Won't Chroma be surprised?" he thought, signaling the musicians to stop. "I'll wake him now."

But, instead of stopping, they continued to play even louder than before, until each color became more brilliant than he thought possible. Milo shielded his eyes with one hand and waved the other desperately, but the colors continued to grow brighter and brighter and brighter, until an even more curious thing began to happen.

As Milo frantically conducted, the sky changed slowly from blue to tan and then to a rich magenta red. Flurries of light-green snow began to fall, and the leaves on the trees and bushes turned a vivid orange.

All the flowers suddenly appeared black, the gray rocks became a lovely soft chartreuse, and even peacefully sleeping Tock changed from brown to a magnificent ultramarine. Nothing was the color it should have been, and yet, the more he tried to straighten things out, the worse they became.

"I wish I hadn't started," he thought unhappily as a pale-blue blackbird flew by. "There doesn't seem to be any way to stop them."

He tried very hard to do everything just the way Chroma had done, but nothing worked. The musicians played on, faster and faster, and the purple sun raced quickly across the sky. In less than a minute it had set once more in the west and then, without any pause, risen again in the east. The sky was now quite yellow and the grass a charming shade of lavender. Seven times the sun rose and almost as quickly disappeared as the colors kept changing. In just a few minutes a whole week had gone by.

At last the exhausted Milo, afraid to call for help and on the verge of tears, dropped his hands to his sides. The orchestra stopped. The colors disappeared, and once again it was night. The time was 5:27 A.M.

"Wake up, everybody! Time for the sunrise!" he shouted with relief, and quickly jumped from the music stand.

"What a marvelous rest," said Chroma, striding to the podium. "I feel as though I'd slept for a week. My, my, I see we're a little late this morning. I'll have to cut my lunch hour short by four minutes."

He tapped for attention, and this time the dawn proceeded perfectly.

"You did a fine job," he said, patting Milo on the head. "Someday I'll let you conduct the orchestra yourself."

Tock wagged his tail proudly, but Milo didn't say a word, and to this day no one knows of the lost week but the few people who happened to be awake at 5:23 on that very strange morning. . . .

MATH CONNECTIONS

Estimation
Multiplication
Measurement
Fractions

Precycle It!

FROM 50 Simple Things Kids Can Do to Save the Earth
BY THE EARTHWORKS GROUP

This selection focuses on the amount of excess packaging that winds up as garbage. As a follow-up activity, students may wish to monitor the amount of packaging that gets thrown away in their home for a week.

Take A Guess.

Over half of the plastic we buy and throw away each year is just packaging. What happens to it when it's thrown away?

A) Nothing—it just sits there and clutters up the Earth
B) It gets up and starts dancing
C) It watches TV

Did you ever stop to think that when you buy something packaged in plastic or cardboard, you're actually buying and paying for the thing *plus garbage?*

It sounds ridiculous, doesn't it? But that's what happens. You tear off the packaging and stuff it right in the garbage!

If it's plastic packaging, it's made from one of the Earth's greatest buried treasures—oil. It's been underground for millions of years! . . . And it may have even been part of a dinosaur once! Think about that!

If we turn oil into plastic, we can never change it back; it can never be part of the Earth again.

So whenever you buy a toy, some food, or anything . . . you have a terrific chance to help the Earth! Look around. See how things are packaged. Make careful choices. You can do it!

Did You Know
• Each American throws away about 60 pounds of plastic packaging every year! Think about how much *you* weigh. Now think about how much 60 pounds is. That's a lot of plastic.
• Americans use *2.5 million* plastic bottles every *hour*. Can you believe it? And most of them get thrown away.
• Remember when we talked about how our garbage dumps are filling up? Well, about 1/3 of all that garbage is packaging. Less packaging means less garbage.

What You Can Do
• Look for ways to practice *precycling*. That means buying things which come in packages that can be recycled (not turned into garbage), or are made of materials that have *already* been recycled.
• For example: If you go food shopping with your family, buy eggs in cardboard, not Styrofoam, cartons. (Then reuse the cartons for art projects.)
• Some cereal, crackers and cookies come in boxes made of recycled cardboard. It's easy to spot them: recycled cardboard is gray on the inside.
• Many toymakers use expensive packaging to make their toys seem better than they are. Sometimes there's more to the package than to the toy itself! Check it out.

See For Yourself
• Keep a big bag or box handy to collect the packaging you throw away. You'll be surprised at how much you collect in a few days.

(Answer: A. Plastic will be sitting around for hundreds of years, at least! What a mess!)

Use with Chapter 7, Lesson 3

MATH CONNECTIONS

Decimals
Multiplication
Division
Money

Baseballs for Sale

FROM Max Malone Makes A Million
BY CHARLOTTE HERMAN

Max Malone wants to get rich quick. He's willing to work hard, but none of his schemes seem to work. But Max and his friend Gordy don't give up.

"**A**ustin Healy is having his appendix out today," said Max.

"Yeah, I heard about that," said Gordy. "He threw up all his popcorn last night. Too bad he has to miss Dusty Field on Friday."

Max and Gordy were on their way to Toys for Less. They each had two dollars and fifty cents to spend at the store's Giant Summer Clearance Sale.

When they reached the store, they saw signs on all the windows:

SUMMER BLOWOUT!

Prices Slashed!

25–50% Off Selected Items

"I hope we find some good stuff," said Max as they went inside. They walked past the first few counters, which displayed the inexpensive toys and prizes like the ones they'd bought for their carnival. They were looking for more expensive, quality items. Max hoped to find something worth five dollars for half off. Then he would have enough money. He didn't have to look far. The idea hit him the moment he saw them.

"That's it!" he cried out. "That's perfect."

"What's it? What's perfect?" asked Gordy.

Max pointed to a box of rubber baseballs. A sign on the box read: 20 CENTS EACH.

"Don't you see? We buy these baseballs for twenty cents each. Then we sell them at a higher price to people who want Dusty Field's autograph."

"You're a genius," said Gordy, slapping Max on the back. "That's a great idea. All we have to do is figure out how many balls we can buy for our five dollars." He looked up at the ceiling and concentrated. "Let's see now. If each ball costs twenty cents, and we have five dollars . . . . I forget . . . . Do we divide or multiply?"

"We divide," said Max, writing and erasing in the air. "Twenty cents into five dollars . . ."

Gordy was impressed. "How many can we buy, Max?"

"Hold your horses. I have to move the decimals."

Max continued writing, but he stopped suddenly in midair. "Wait. I have another idea. First we have to see the manager."

Max's eyes searched the store for someone who looked like a manager. He saw a young woman walking around, giving orders to the workers.

"That must be the manager," he said, walking toward her.

Gordy followed, and a few minutes later Max was asking, "Excuse me, but are you the manager?"

"Yes," said the young woman. "Can I help you?"

"I was wondering," said Max. "If we buy those rubber baseballs in quantity, how much will you sell them for?"

The manager looked up at the ceiling the way Gordy had done. Max waited nervously.

"How much do you want to spend?" she asked after a while.

"Five dollars—including tax," he answered.

"I'll tell you what. Summer's over. And I need the space more than I need the baseballs. For five dollars—including tax—you can have the whole box. There should be close to fifty balls in there."

"Fifty?" Max cried out. "It's a deal."

"Forty-eight baseballs at fifty cents apiece. We'll really make a fortune, almost," said Max.

"Forty-six," Gordy corrected. "We have to save two for ourselves."

It was Friday morning, and Max and Gordy, each carrying a bag of baseballs, were on their way to the sporting-goods store. It was only nine thirty, and the store didn't open until ten. But they wanted to get there early so they wouldn't miss a single person.

A long line of kids was already forming in front of the store. "Everyone wants to meet Dusty Field," said Max.

"My father said his autograph might become valuable some day," said Gordy. "A real collectible."

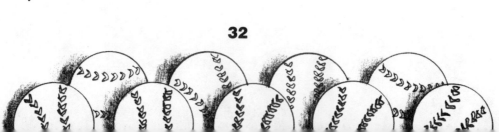

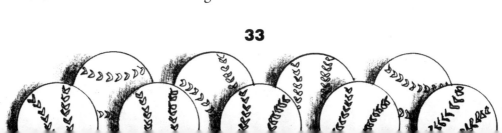

Some of the kids had come prepared with baseballs or mitts for autographing. Some had autograph books, and a few were holding scraps of paper. But most of them didn't have anything. Max was sure that lots of people would want the baseballs. Well, he was almost sure. He knew he should start selling right away, but he couldn't make himself move. His legs felt like spaghetti. Thinking about selling had been a lot easier than actually doing it. There were so many people. What if nobody wanted to buy any baseballs? What if he and Gordy got chased away by the store owner? Or the police?

Rosalie had warned him about that. She said that he and Gordy needed a license to sell the baseballs. Max didn't know if she knew what she was talking about. He had heard of a dog license. And a license to drive a car. But never a license to sell baseballs.

"What are we waiting for?" asked Gordy.

"You go first," said Max.

"No, you first. It was your idea."

"We'll go together," said Max. He dipped his hand into the bag and pulled out two baseballs. He forced himself to walk along the line of kids and call out, "Baseballs for sale. Just fifty cents." He waved the balls around so everyone could see them. A few people glanced in Max's direction, but turned away.

Gordy, in the meantime, was calling out, "Get your baseballs autographed by Dusty Field. Just fifty cents. Sure to become a collectible."

To his surprise, Max saw that a few kids actually went over to buy some balls from Gordy. Max then took up the call.

"Get your baseballs autographed by Dusty. Just fifty cents. Sure to become valuable." He didn't want to copy Gordy exactly.

A girl with an autograph book came over to buy a ball. "A baseball is better than an autograph book," she said, handing him the money.

A mother with a small boy came by. "I didn't even think to bring anything that Dusty could sign. This is such a good idea."

Some kids with scraps of paper stuffed the papers into their pockets, or dumped them into trash cans. Then they bought baseballs from Max.

Max was having a great time. He could see that Gordy was too. The scene was just as he had pictured. He was selling what people wanted to buy. And the more he sold, the more confident he became. He even began singing "Take Me Out to the Ball Game." The crowd in front of the store joined in.

Suddenly Max stopped singing. Someone inside the store, the manager probably, was standing at the door, staring at Max. Max stared back, and then looked away. This was it! He and Gordy would be asked to leave. He should have known it was too good to last.

The manager opened the door, and the kids pushed their way in. But the manager disappeared. He was nowhere in sight. Neither were the police. Max decided that if someone came and told him to stop, he would. But until then, he would keep on selling.

He stopped customers before they went into the store. "Get your baseball for Dusty Field's autograph. Fifty cents." Or, "How about a baseball for Dusty's autograph?" Most people were eager to buy.

Dusty was going to be signing autographs until noon. But by eleven, Max and Gordy had sold all their baseballs. All except the two they had saved for themselves.

"I can't believe it," said Max when he and Gordy were waiting in line to meet Dusty. "We sold them all. I thought our goose was cooked when I saw the manager staring at me." Max's mother always used that expression — "my goose was cooked" — even though she had never cooked a goose in her life.

"I can't believe we're getting Dusty's autograph," said Gordy. "I wish the line would move faster. Dusty's hand will get all worn out from shaking hands before he even gets to us."

At last it was Max and Gordy's turn to meet Dusty. Dusty was tall and thin and had a friendly smile. He wasn't wearing a uniform. Just jeans and a T-shirt. But he looked like a ball player anyway.

Max and Dusty shook hands. Dusty said, "Nice to meet you."

But Max couldn't think of anything great to say except, "Would you sign this ball to Max?"

"Sure thing," said Dusty, and he signed the ball, *To my pal Max. Dusty Field.*

"Wow! Thanks, Dusty."

Gordy couldn't think of anything to say either. So he handed Dusty his baseball and said, "I'm Gordy."

Dusty signed, *To my pal Gordy. Dusty Field.*

"Wow!" said Gordy.

"This was a great day," said Max.

"Let's go home and split up the money," said Gordy.

"We made a ton," said Max. "And all because we knew the market. We went where the people were. And we bought in quantity. Just like Austin . . ."

Austin. Max had forgotten all about him. Little Austin Healy, who was home with a scar where his appendix should have been. Austin, who was looking forward to meeting Dusty Field. Why, if it weren't for Austin, Max would never have known about Dusty. He and Gordy would never have bought the balls. They never would've made all that money.

"We can't go home yet," said Max. "There's something we have to do first." He led the way to the baseball section of the store. And there, in a bin, were baseballs. Real league baseballs. They cost three dollars, but Max didn't care. He picked one up and showed it to Gordy.

"For Austin," he said.

"We'll get it autographed by Dusty," said Gordy.

They bought the ball and waited in line again.

"Let's see," said Gordy, looking up at the ceiling. "Not counting what we spent on Austin, if we sold forty-six balls at fifty cents each . . ."

"This time we multiply," said Max.

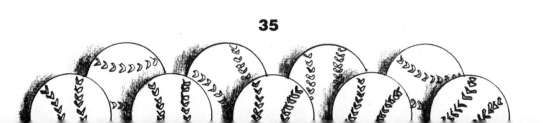

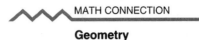
Said Mrs. Isosceles Tri

BY CLINTON BROOKS BURGESS

This poem may help students who are having difficulty classifying geometric shapes visualize an isosceles triangle.

Said Mrs. Isosceles Tri,
"That I'm sharp I've no wish to deny;
　　But I do not dare
　　To be perfectly square —
I'm sure if I did I should die!"

Use with Chapter 9, Lesson 13

⋀⋀⋀ MATH CONNECTIONS

Measurement
Estimation

⋀⋀⋀ CULTURAL CONNECTION

Chinese Fable

Buying Shoes

FROM 100 Ancient Chinese Fables
TRANSLATED BY K. L. KIU

What would your students do if they found themselves in the man's situation?
Would they trust their feet or the measurement?

A man of the state of Zheng wanted to buy a pair of shoes. He measured his foot and put the measurement on a chair. When he set out for the market he forgot to bring it along. It was after he had found the pair he wanted that this occurred to him.

"I forgot the measurement," said he.

He went home to get it but when he returned the market had broken up and he did not get his shoes after all.

"Why didn't you try on the shoes with your feet?" he was asked.

"I'd rather trust the measurement than trust myself."

Hanfeizi

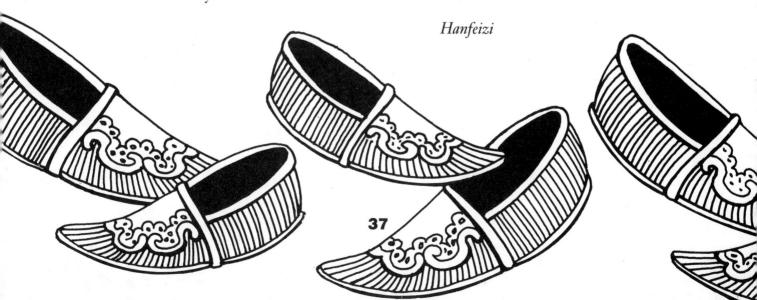

37

MATH CONNECTIONS

Fractions
Addition

CULTURAL CONNECTION

**Northwestern Native
American Recipes**

Huckleberry Fritters and Cranberry Fritters

FROM *Spirit of the Harvest: North American Indian Cooking*
BY BEVERLY COX AND MARTIN JACOBS

Huckleberry Fritters

Large supplies of berries were gathered and preserved by all Northwestern tribes. Berry-picking grounds were clan owned, and outsiders would have to ask permission to pick there. Four varieties of huckleberries were especially enjoyed: coastal, tall blue forest, black mountain, and evergreen. To gather the tiny black coastal huckleberry, Lummi women used wooden combs to sweep both leaves and berries into their baskets. At home, the contents were rolled down the wetted surface of a tilted cedar plank, allowing the berries to collect in waiting baskets while the leaves stuck to the wet plank. Today, berries are boiled with sugar and put up in mason jars, or stored raw, covered with sugar. This latter preparation makes excellent fritters.

2 cups huckleberries or blueberries	$1\frac{1}{4}$ teaspoons baking powder
3 cups unbleached flour	3 eggs
$\frac{1}{2}$ cup sugar	$\frac{1}{2}$ cup water

Oil, for deep-frying

Wash berries and allow to drain. Sift dry ingredients together into a mixing bowl. Beat eggs with water until foamy. Mix quickly into dry ingredients. Fold in berries. Heat oil or shortening in deep, heavy skillet to 350°F. on a deep-frying thermometer or until a bread cube dropped in the oil turns golden brown in 1 minute.

Drop batter by tablespoonfuls into the hot oil. Turn fritters frequently so that they brown to a deep golden brown on all sides. Drain on paper towels and serve hot. Makes 2 dozen.

Cranberry Fritters

The dough used for making the fritters in this recipe is a sweetened version of the basic fry bread dough popular with Native Americans in all regions. The Northwestern idea of forming the dough around a firm berry is interesting and fun.

$\frac{3}{4}$	cup fresh cranberries
$1\frac{1}{2}$	cups unbleached flour
$\frac{3}{4}$	cup granulated sugar
1	tablespoon baking powder
$\frac{1}{4}$	teaspoon salt
$\frac{1}{2}$	cup plus 1 tablespoon milk
$\frac{1}{4}$	cup dark brown sugar

Oil, for deep-frying
Confectioners' sugar (optional)

Wash cranberries and dry on paper towels. Sift dry ingredients together and mix in milk gradually to form a stiff dough. With well-floured hands, pinch off 1 teaspoon of dough and make an indentation. Sprinkle a little brown sugar in the indentation and place a cranberry in the center. Roll dough around the berry. Balls should be about the size of a large marble. Heat oil in a deep, heavy kettle until the temperature reaches 375°F. on a deep-frying thermometer or until a bread cube turns golden brown in 30 to 40 seconds. Drop fritter balls into the hot fat and fry, turning until they are deep golden brown on all sides. Drain on paper towels. If desired, shake confectioners' sugar over the fritters just before serving. Makes 3 dozen.

MATH CONNECTIONS

Fractions
Addition
Multiplication
Number Sense

CULTURAL CONNECTION

Folktale from Jamaica

Anansi and the Plantains

FROM *Anansi the Spider Man*
TOLD BY PHILIP M. SHERLOCK

The Anansi tales have spread from West Africa to the Caribbean and the United States. When Anansi senses danger, he changes from a man into a spider.

*I*t was market day, but Anansi had no money. He sat at the door of his cottage and watched Tiger and Kisander the cat, Dog and Goat, and a host of others hurrying to the market to buy and sell. He had nothing to sell, for he had not done any work in his field. Turtle had won the few coins that he had saved in the broken calabash that he kept hidden under his bed. How was he to find food for his wife Crooky and for the children? Above all, how was he to find food for himself?

Soon Crooky came to the door and spoke to him. "You must go out now, Anansi, and find something for us to eat. We have nothing for lunch, nothing for dinner, and tomorrow is Sunday. What are we going to do without a scrap of food in the house?"

"I am going out to work for some food," said Anansi. "Do not worry. Every day you have seen me go with nothing and come home with something. You watch and see!"

Anansi walked about until noon and found nothing, so he lay down to sleep under the shade of a large mango tree. There he slept and waited until the sun began to go down. Then, in the cool of the evening he set off for home. He walked slowly, for he was ashamed to be going home empty-handed. He was asking himself what he was to do, and where he would find food for the children, when he came face to face with his old friend

Rat going home with a large bunch of plantains on his head. The bunch was so big and heavy that Brother Rat had to bend down almost to the earth to carry it.

Anansi's eyes shone when he saw the plantains, and he stopped to speak to his friend Rat.

"How are you, my friend Rat? I haven't seen you for a very long time."

"Oh, I am staggering along, staggering along," said Rat. "And how are you—and the family?"

Anansi put on his longest face, so long that his chin almost touched his toes. He groaned and shook his head. "Ah, Brother Rat," he said, "times are hard, times are very hard. I can hardly find a thing to eat from one day to the next." At this tears came into his eyes, and he went on:

"I walked all yesterday. I have been walking all today and I haven't found a yam or a plantain." He glanced for a moment at the large bunch of plantains. "Ah, Br'er Rat, the children will have nothing but water for supper tonight."

"I am sorry to hear that," said Rat; "very sorry indeed. I know how I would feel if I had to go home to my wife and children without any food."

"Without even a plantain," said Anansi, and again he looked for a moment at the plantains.

Br'er Rat looked at the bunch of plantains, too. He put it on the ground and looked at it in silence.

Anansi said nothing, but he moved toward the plantains. They drew him like a magnet. He could not take his eyes away from them, except for an occasional quick glance at Rat's face. Rat said nothing. Anansi said nothing. They both looked at the plantains.

Then at last Anansi spoke. "My friend," he said, "what a lovely bunch of plantains! Where did you get it in these hard times?"

"It's all that I had left in my field, Anansi. This bunch must last until the peas are ready, and they are not ready yet."

"But they will be ready soon," said Anansi, "they will be ready soon. Brother Rat, give me one or two of the plantains. The children have eaten nothing, and they have only water for supper."

"All right, Anansi," said Rat. "Just wait a minute."

Rat counted all the plantains carefully and then said, "Well, perhaps, Br'er Anansi, perhaps!" Then he counted them again and finally he broke off the four smallest plantains and gave them to Anansi.

"Thank you," said Anansi, "thank you, my good friend. But, Rat, it's four plantains; and there are five of us in the family—my wife, the three children, and myself."

Rat took no notice of this. He only said, "Help me to put this bunch of plantains on my head, Br'er Anansi, and do not try to break off any more."

So Anansi had to help Rat to put the bunch of plantains back on his head. Rat went off, walking slowly because of the weight of the bunch. Then Anansi set off for his home. He could walk quickly because the four plantains were not a heavy burden. When he got to his home he handed the four plantains to Crooky, his wife, and told her to roast them. He went outside and sat down in the shade of the mango tree until Crooky called out to say that the plantains were ready.

Anansi went back inside. There were the four plantains, nicely roasted. He took up one and gave it to the girl. He gave one each to the two boys. He gave the last and biggest plantain to his wife. After that he sat down empty-handed and very, very sad-looking, and his wife said to him, "Don't you want some of the plantains?"

"No," said Anansi, with a deep sigh. "There are only enough for four of us. I'm hungry, too, because I haven't had anything to eat; but there are just enough for you."

The little child asked, "Aren't you hungry, Papa?"

"Yes, my child, I am hungry, but you are too little. You cannot find food for yourselves. It's better for me to remain hungry as long as your stomachs are filled."

"No, Papa," shouted the children, "you must have half of my plantain." They all broke their plantains in two, and each one gave Anansi a half. When Crooky saw what was happening she gave Anansi half of her plantain, too. So, in the end, Anansi got more than anyone, just as usual.

Bird Watching

BY MYRA COHN LIVINGSTON

*Created especially for this anthology, Myra Cohn Livingston's poem will enhance
students' understanding of ratio.*

Up in the bush is a tiny nest,
that's where the hummingbird likes it best.

Out in the trees the mockingbirds call;
Three built nests just over the wall,

And in the morning, yesterday,
I saw four crows and two bluejays.

Those were the birds I counted — ten.
Will ever the same birds come again?

43

One Inch Tall

FROM Where the Sidewalk Ends
BY SHEL SILVERSTEIN

What do your students think the world would be like if they were one-inch tall?
Would they rather be one-hundred feet tall?

If you were only one inch tall, you'd ride a worm to school.
The teardrop of a crying ant would be your swimming pool.
A crumb of cake would be a feast
And last you seven days at least,
A flea would be a frightening beast
If you were one inch tall.

If you were only one inch tall, you'd walk beneath the door,
And it would take about a month to get down to the store.
A bit of fluff would be your bed,
You'd swing upon a spider's thread,
And wear a thimble on your head
If you were one inch tall.

You'd surf across the kitchen sink upon a stick of gum.
You couldn't hug your mama, you'd just have to hug her thumb.
You'd run from people's feet in fright,
To move a pen would take all night,
(This poem took fourteen years to write —
'Cause I'm just one inch tall).

INDEX

•INDEX BY TITLE•

Anansi and the Plantains, 40

Baseballs for Sale, 31
Bird Watching, 43
Buying Shoes, 37

Distances, 6
Don't Can It!, 22

Halfway Up the Skies, 20
Huckleberry and Cranberry Fritters, 38

I Don't Have the Words, 11

Melisande, 15

Numbers, 2

One Inch Tall, 44

Peter Anthony, 3
Phantom Tollbooth, The, 24
Precycle It!, 29

Said Mrs. Isosceles Tri, 36
Sticks of Truth, 9

Too Clever Is Not Clever, 4

•INDEX OF MATH CONNECTIONS•

ADDITION

Anansi and the Plantains, 40
Bird Watching, 43
Huckleberry and Cranberry Fritters, 38
I Don't Have the Words, 11
Too Clever Is Not Clever, 4

DECIMALS

Baseballs for Sale, 31
I Don't Have the Words, 11

DIVISION

Baseballs for Sale, 31
Don't Can It!, 22
Halfway Up the Skies, 20
Too Clever Is Not Clever, 4

ESTIMATION

Buying Shoes, 37
Melisande, 15
Precycle It!, 29

FRACTIONS

Anansi and the Plantains, 40
Huckleberry and Cranberry Fritters, 38
Precycle It!, 29

GEOMETRY

Halfway Up the Skies, 20
Said Mrs. Isosceles Tri, 36

MEASUREMENT

Buying Shoes, 37
Distances, 6
Melisande, 15
One Inch Tall, 44
Precycle It!, 29
Sticks of Truth, The, 9

MONEY

Baseballs for Sale, 31

MULTIPLICATION

Anansi and the Plantains, 40
Baseballs for Sale, 31
Don't Can It!, 22
Halfway Up the Skies, 20
Melisande, 15
Precycle It!, 29
Too Clever Is Not Clever, 4

NUMBER PATTERNS

Don't Can It!, 22

NUMBER SENSE

Anansi and the Plantains, 40
Numbers, 2
Peter Anthony, 3
Too Clever Is Not Clever, 4

PROPORTION

One Inch Tall, 44

RATIO

Bird Watching, 43

SUBTRACTION

I Don't Have the Words, 11
Too Clever Is Not Clever, 4

TIME

Distances, 6
Phantom Tollbooth, The, 24
Sticks of Truth, The, 9

•INDEX BY CATEGORY•

STORIES

Anansi and the Plantains, 40
Baseballs for Sale, 31
Buying Shoes, 37
Halfway Up the Skies, 20
Melisande, 15
Phantom Tollbooth, The, 24
Sticks of Truth, The, 9
Too Clever Is Not Clever, 4

NONFICTION

Don't Can It!, 22
Huckleberry and Cranberry Fritters, 38
Precycle It!, 29

BIOGRAPHY

Distances, 6
I Don't Have the Words, 11

POEMS

Bird Watching, 43
Numbers, 2
One Inch Tall, 44
Peter Anthony, 3
Said Mrs. Isosceles Tri, 36

•INDEX BY AUTHOR•

Ausubel, Nathan, 4

Burgess, Clinton Brooks, 36

Cox, Beverly, 38

EarthWorks Group, The, 22, 29

Farjeon, Eleanor, 2

Herman, Charlotte, 31

Jacobs, Martin, 38
Juster, Norton, 24

Kiu, K. L., 20, 37
Knudson, R. R., 6

Liatsos, Sandra, 3
Livingston, Myra Cohn, 43

Nesbit, E., 15

Shannon, George, 9
Sherlock, Philip, 40
Silverstein, Shel, 44

Walker, Paul Robert, 11

•INDEX OF SELECTIONS BY CONTINENT•

AFRICA

West Africa
Anansi and the Plantains, 40
Retold by Philip Sherlock

ASIA

China
Buying Shoes, 37
Translated by K. L. Kiu

Halfway Up the Skies, 20
Translated by K. L. Kiu

India
Sticks of Truth, The, 9
Retold by George Shannon

EUROPE

Too Clever Is Not Clever, 4
Retold by Nathan Ausubel

England
Numbers, 2
By Eleanor Farjeon

NORTH AMERICA

Native American
Huckleberry and Cranberry
Fritters, 38 *(Northwest)*
By Beverly Cox and Martin Jacobs

Puerto Rico
I Don't Have the Words, 11
By Paul Robert Walker

Jamaica, Trinidad
Anansi and the Plantains, 40
Retold by Philip Sherlock

North American Contemporary
Anansi and the Plantains, 40
Retold by Philip Sherlock

Baseballs for Sale, 31
By Charlotte Herman

Bird Watching, 43
By Myra Cohn Livingston

Distances, 6
By R. R. Knudson

Don't Can It!, 22
By the EarthWorks Group

Huckleberry and Cranberry Fritters, 38
By Beverly Cox and Martin Jacobs

I Don't Have the Words, 11
By Paul Robert Walker

Melisande, 15
By E. Nesbit

One Inch Tall, 44
By Shel Silverstein

Peter Anthony, 3
By Sandra Liatsos

Phantom Tollbooth, The, 24
By Norton Juster

Precycle It!, 29
By the EarthWorks Group

Said Mrs. Isosceles Tri, 36
By Clinton Brooks Burgess

Sticks of Truth, The, 9
Retold by George Shannon

Too Clever Is Not Clever, 4
Retold by Nathan Ausubel

ACKNOWLEDGMENTS *(continued)*

Excerpt from THE PHANTOM TOLLBOOTH by Norton Juster. Text copyright © 1961 by Norton Juster. Copyright renewed 1989 by Norton Juster. Reprinted by permission of Random House, Inc.

"Bird Watching" by Myra Cohn Livingston. Copyright © 1993 by Myra Cohn Livingston. Used by permission of Marian Reiner for the author.

"Peter Anthony" by Sandra Liatsos. Copyright © 1993 by Sandra Liatsos. Used by permission of Marian Reiner for the author.

"Huckleberry Fritters" and "Cranberry Fritters" from NORTH AMERICAN INDIAN COOKING by Beverly Cox and Martin Jacobs. Text copyright © 1991 by Beverly Cox and Martin Jacobs. Reprinted by permission of Stewart, Tabori & Chang, Inc.

"Halfway Up the Skies" and "Buying Shoes" from 100 ANCIENT CHINESE FABLES translated by K. L. Kiu. Reprinted by permission of K. L. Kiu.

Cursive Writing *words*

lion   lamp   leaf

MAPLE PRESS

Cursive
Writing
words

MAPLE PRESS

Copyright © Publisher

Published in 2016 by

MAPLE PRESS PRIVATE LIMITED

sales office A 63, Sector 58, Noida 201 301, U.P., India

phone +91 120 455 3581, 455 3583

email info@maplepress.co.in

website www.maplepress.co.in